T0208135

Sex, Health, and Long Life

Sex, Health, and Long Life

MANUALS OF TAOIST PRACTICE

TRANSLATED BY

THOMAS CLEARY

SHAMBHALA

Boston & London

1999

SHAMBHALA PUBLICATIONS, INC.
HORTICULTURAL HALL
300 MASSACHUSETTS AVENUE
BOSTON, MASSACHUSETTS 02115
http://www.shambhala.com

♾ This edition is printed on acid-free paper that meets the American National Standards Institute z39.48 Standard. Distributed in the United States by Random House, Inc., and in Canada by Random House of Canada Ltd

Library of Congress Cataloging-in-Publication Data

Sex, health, and long life: manuals of Taoist practice/
    translated by Thomas Cleary.
        p.   cm.—(Shambhala pocket classics)
    Translated from Chinese.
    Includes bibliographical references.
    ISBN 1-57062-059-8 (Shambhala Pocket Classics)
    ISBN 1-57062-433-X (pbk.: alk. paper)
    1. Hygiene, Taoist.   2. Hygiene, Sexual.   3. Health.
    4. Longevity.   I. Cleary, Thomas F., 1949– .   II. Series.
    RA781.S49   1995   94-22555
    613—dc20   CIP

BVG 01

Contents

Translator's Introduction

"The human body," according to an old Taoist book, "consists of vitality, energy, and spirit." In Taoist health science, vitality, energy, and spirit are called the Three Treasures, and their care and cultivation are considered the basis of health, happiness, and long life.

In simple terms, *vitality* refers to sexuality, *energy* refers to strength, *spirit* refers to intelligence. The Taoist alchemy of well-being is the science of combining these three elements in such a way as to maximize the benefits of natural potential, harmonizing instinct, emotion, and reason.

Within the broad spectrum of Taoist traditions, which include a very wide range of interests and studies, one of the earliest movements to emphasize conscious exercise of the connection between physical and mental well-being is found in the so-called Huang-Lao school.

The name of this school is taken from the names of Huang Di, the legendary Yellow Emperor of the late-middle third millennium BCE, to whom a lot of health and sex lore is attributed, and Lao Tzu, the "Ancient Master," legendary author of the work known as *De Dao Jing,* later recast as *Tao Te Ching.*

Recent archeological finds in China have unearthed hitherto

unknown texts of this tradition, presented here together for the first time in English, showing the comprehensive scope of the Huang-Lao approach to physical and mental hygiene.

The five texts translated here were part of the famous Mawangdui finds of 1973–74. The first three, *Ten Questions, Joining Yin and Yang*, and *Talk on Supreme Guidance for the World*, deal specifically with physical health and sex lore, including diet, exercise, sleep, and lovemaking technique. The last two, entitled *A Course in Effectiveness* and *A Course in Guidance*, concentrate on the psychological factors of good health and well-being, especially the reduction of stress and cultivation of wholesome social relations.

Ten Questions takes the form of questions and answers on health lore between legendary rulers and Taoist adepts. General recommendations include prolonged sexual intercourse and control of ejaculation; exercises in mindful breathing; enhancement of the diet with items such as milk, eggs, nuts, leeks, and spices; adequate sleep; and moderate intake of wine.

Joining Yin and Yang is devoted to sexual techniques and the health benefits of blissful intercourse. The importance of mood, sensitive foreplay, thorough arousal, and complete satisfaction of the female are given particular emphasis. While control of the male ejaculation is considered essential, the forced methods later devised by Taoist sexologists for this purpose are not represented in this text, which instead implies a more general approach involving cultivation of attention, carefulness, and pacing.

Talk on Supreme Guidance for the World goes into more detailed reasoning on the relationship between sex and health. Again the emphasis is on physical and mental energization by multiple complete acts of love without male ejaculation. Numerous successive stages of physical and mental bliss are identified and described, and general outlines of sexual function and dysfunction are followed by recapitulations of techniques, methods, and styles of sexual intercourse.

A Course in Effectiveness (De Jing) and *A Course in Guidance (Dao Jing)* are titled separately, in this manner, and also as a set: *Courses in Effectiveness and Guidance (De Dao Jing)*. This is a long-lost version of the famous *Tao Te Ching;* both are interpretations of even older lore, but that of the *De Dao Jing,* in the Huang-Lao tradition of Taoism, is more down-to-earth than the comparatively abstract and mystical interpretations of ancient lore in the *Tao Te Ching.*

The teachings of *Courses in Effectiveness and Guidance* approach health and long life through radical relief of harmful stress resulting from habits such as compulsive anxiety, paranoia, aggression. Moods of serenity, buoyancy, compassion, and freedom are prescribed for both direct and indirect benefits, as they enhance individual well-being and also interpersonal and professional relationships. Mental postures and contemplative exercises conducive to the elimination of toxic feelings and the development of therapeutic feelings are outlined throughout both courses of this revered text.

TEN QUESTIONS

1

THE YELLOW EMPEROR asked a Celestial Teacher, "How do beings operate? How do plants and trees grow? How are the sun and the moon bright?"

The Celestial Teacher said, "Observe the conditions of the sky. Yin and yang are the standards of order; when beings lose this, they do not propagate, but when they have it, they thrive. Ingest yin to solidify yang, and you reach clarity of spirit.

"The way to ingest yin is to fortify your internal organs, strengthen your metabolic functions, so that energy cannot escape the body. When ingesting yin, it is important to be calm, yet sexually aroused. Embrace at the peak of excitement, penetrate repeatedly without ejaculation, and sexual arousal grows, answered by moans and sighs.

"Take deep breaths, no more than five, breathing through the mouth and taking energy into the heart, so that it fills the limbs, whereupon pure saliva is produced. Swallow this, no more than five times, making sure the taste is sweet, directing it to the internal organs, and the body will quickly become passive.

"Drive the energy into your flesh and skin, even to the tips of your hairs, and your pores and circulatory channels will open. The sexual liquid is then present, causing the male erection to stand up firm and unwilting.

"Eat and drink to suit the body.

"This is called the method of restoring what has been depleted, leading to clarity of spirit."

This is a Celestial Teacher's method of ingesting the energy of the spirit.

2

THE YELLOW EMPEROR asked Dacheng, "What lack causes people's complexions to become coarse and dusky, dull and sallow? What can people get that will make the texture of the skin beautiful, clear, and lustrous?"

Dacheng replied, "If you want clear skin, observe the caterpillar. The way the caterpillar eats is directly connected to yin and yang; when it eats greenery it turns green, and when it eats yellow it turns yellow. It is your diet that alters colors.

"You must eat yin on a regular basis; add cedar nuts, which are excellent, and drink the milk of running animals. Then you can fend off old age, restore strength, and glow with vitality.

"Engage in plenty of sexual intercourse. Eat of flying birds, such as sparrow eggs and roosters. Roosters have male hormones in them; if you consume this, your 'jade rod' will stand up again. When erect, its strength is sufficient and ready for the 'jade opening'; when fully aroused, go ahead.

"Encourage it with sparrow eggs; but if you do not get a strong enough erection, put the eggs in wheat gruel or malt. If you eat this, you can recover from impotence."

This is Dacheng's way of curing impotence by ingesting the vitality of birds.

3

THE YELLOW EMPEROR asked Cao Ao, "What is the lack from which people die? What enables them to live?"

Cao Ao replied, "The mating of female and male, and the taking of that vitality.

"When you engage in sexual intercourse, make gentle physical movements. When you can arouse the woman's body and make her pant, giggle, sigh, moan, and cry out, then you ejaculate into her. Those who are drained can thus be revitalized, those who are robust can thus be enabled to prolong their vitality, while those who are old can thus be enabled to extend their lives.

"The way to extend life involves watching over the closing off of the flow of semen. When the semen is locked up and stored in a timely manner, then spiritual clarity comes and builds up; and when it builds up, it inevitably becomes evident. Locking up the semen to stabilize vitality ensures that the supply of sexual fluid is never exhausted. Then diseases do not afflict you, so you can live a long time.

"The way to embrace a woman requires peaceful serenity of heart, so the body and the mood calm one another.

"So it is said, embrace once without ejaculating, and your

eyes and ears will be clear; embrace twice without ejaculating, and your voice will be clear. Embrace three times without ejaculating, and your skin will be lustrous; embrace four times without ejaculating, and your back and sides won't be susceptible to injury. Embrace five times without ejaculating, and your gluteus and thighs will be strong and muscular; embrace six times without ejaculating, and all your energy channels will flow freely. Embrace seven times without ejaculating, and you will never die ahead of your time; embrace eight times without ejaculating, and you can enjoy long life. Embrace nine times without ejaculating, and you attain to clarity of spirit."

This is Cao Ao's way of embracing women to cultivate spiritual energy.

4

THE YELLOW EMPEROR asked Rong Cheng, "When people originally propagate, taking on forms, what do they have that enables them to live? Once they take on physical form, what loss makes them die? In what epoch did humanity come to have likes and dislikes, to have early death or long life? I would like to hear the reasons why people's energy expands and contracts, slackens and tightens."

Rong Cheng replied, "If you want to live a long time, then attentively examine the ways of heaven and earth. The energy of heaven is used up monthly and replenished monthly; thus it can live long. The energy of earth has cold and hot seasons each year, and complementary terrains; thus the earth can endure and not disintegrate. You must examine the conditions of heaven and earth, then put them into operation in your own body.

"There are intelligible indications, but even sages are not capable of understanding them; only masters of the Way can know them.

"The quintessence of heaven and earth arises where there is no sign, grows where there is no form, and matures where there is no body. Those who realize it live long, those who miss it die young.

"Therefore, those who skillfully govern energy and amass vitality build them up imperceptibly. The fountain of vital spirit full, you collect sweet dew to build it up, regularly drinking of pure springs and special wines, getting rid of bad behavior and improving habits. Then the spirit will remain in the body.

"The way to collect energy is to cause it to reach the extremities, so that vitality arises without deficiency. When the upper and lower body are both vitalized, how can chills or fevers occur? The breathing should be deep and prolonged, so that fresh energy is easily maintained.

"Stale energy makes for aging, fresh energy makes for longevity. Therefore, those who are skilled at governing their energy cause stale energy to disperse nightly, and gather fresh energy in the mornings, so as to clear the apertures of the body and replenish the internal organs.

"There are prohibitions in ingesting energy. In spring, avoid polluted warm vapors. In summer, avoid hot, humid air. In autumn, avoid frosty mist. In winter, avoid extreme cold. Avoid these four problems, and deep breathing will make for longevity.

"The aim of morning breathing is that the exhalations should conform to nature, while the inhalations should fill the lungs, as if being stored in a profound abyss. Then old energy will be used up daily and new energy will be replenished daily. Then the physical body will be lustrous and radiant, filled with vitality, and thus able to live long.

"The aim of daytime breathing is that the exhalation and inhalation should be gentle, ears and eyes clear, with a very subtle mood of joy, not suffering internal degeneration, so the body does not die prematurely from illness.

"The aim of nighttime breathing is that respiration be deep, long, and slow, causing the ears not to hear, so one can sleep peacefully. The higher and lower souls rest in the body, so one can live long.

"As for midnight breathing, do not change sleeping positions even if you wake up; breathe deeply and slowly, without force, so that the internal organs are all enlivened, taking long breaths as a rule.

"If you want to make the spirit live long, you must breathe with the structure of the skin. The way to govern energy is to eject the stale and absorb the fresh, blissfully enjoying the good, filling the body with it. This is called amassing vitality.

"There are norms for governing energy. The task is to build up vitality; when vitality is full to overflowing, it is inevitably emitted, and when vitality has been ejaculated it must be replenished. Replenishment of ejaculate is done while in bed.

"Flavorful wines and foods are useful for regulating energy.

"The eyes become bright, the ears become clear, the skin becomes lustrous, the energy channels are filled; sexual vigor arises, enabling one to stand for a long time and journey for long distances, and thus be able to live long."

5

YAO ASKED SHUN, "What is most valuable in the world?"

Shun replied, "Life is most valuable."

Yao asked, "How does one manage life?"

Shun replied, "By close examination and thorough understanding of yin and yang."

Yao asked, "Human beings have nine apertures and twelve main joints, each set in its place; why is it that the sexual organs are there when people are born but lose their function before the body dies?"

Shun replied, "They are not needed for eating and drinking, and not used for planning and thinking. We avoid their names and conceal the organs themselves. They are used very much, without relaxation or moderation; this is why they are born with the body but 'die' before the body dies."

Yao asked, "How do we manage them?"

Shun replied, "By care, education, consideration, and nutrition, making the erection strong yet going about the act in a slow and relaxed manner, not being premature when full of desire, not ejaculating at the peak of pleasure. Vitality will build up, energy will be stored up, and even though one lives to be a hundred one will be healthier than ever."

This is Shun's way of mastering energy through sexual intercourse.

Wang Ziqiao asked Peng Zu, "What is the essence of human energy?"

Peng Zu replied, "No human energy is more essential than sexual energy. When sexual energy is stifled, the hundred channels become ill; if sexual energy is undeveloped, it is impossible to propagate. Therefore longevity is all a matter of sexual energy.

"The preservation of sexual energy goes along with its development. Therefore masters of the Way discovered exercises such as extending the hands downward, massaging the arms, and rubbing the belly to follow yin and yang. First exhale stale energy, then collect energy for the genitals, breathing it into the sexual organ, nourishing the generative organ, nurturing it like a baby.

"When that baby stands up strongly and repeatedly, be careful to avoid impulsive intercourse, so as to develop a good body. When the internal organs are firm, how can illness occur?

"Those who suffer from chronic ailments invariably have leakage of sexual vitality, congestion of energy channels, and emotional instability. They do not understand the Great Way, so living energy leaves them.

"Ordinary people, born in ignorance, rely on shamanic cur-
ers. By the age of seventy they are bent over; complaining of
their problems, they kill themselves. What a pity!

"Wherein lie death and life? Adepts govern them, filling the
lower body, damming the vitality so that energy does not leak
out. When the mind governs death and life, who can cause
any loss? Carefully preserve energy, avoiding loss, and you can
prolong life for ages, enjoying happiness and longevity for ages.

"Longevity comes from storage and accumulation. Those
who are full of life observe heaven above and apply it on earth
below. Those who can do this unfailingly evolve, so they can
be liberated from the body. Those who understand the Great
Way soar beyond the clouds and rise to the immortal realms,
able to travel far as flowing water and high as a flying dragon,
going at high speed without tiring.

". . . Wu Chengzhao made the four seasons his helpers and
heaven and earth his constants. Wu Chengzhao lived together
with yin and yang; yin and yang do not die, and Wu Chengzhao
was on a par with them. So it is with those who have attained
the Way."

EMPEROR PAN GENG asked a very old man, "I have heard that you use sexual contact for strength, and gather the vitality of nature for long life. What should I do to make it possible to practice the Way?"

The old man replied, "You should value that which comes with the body at birth but ages before the body. This will strengthen the weak, extend the life of the short-lived, and cause the poor to have plenty of food.

"The act consists of alternate emptying and replenishing. There are rules for mastering this. First is extending the limbs, straightening the back, and curving the buttocks. Second is relaxing the thighs, moving the genitals, and tightening the anus. Third is closing the eyes and not hearing, gathering energy to fill the brain. Fourth is swallowing saliva and drinking milk. Fifth is all vitalities rising and massing into a great luminous clarity. Stop when you reach the fifth, and your vital spirit will grow happier day by day."

This is a very old man's way of ingesting spiritual energy through sexual contact.

8

Yu ASKED SHI GUI, "I have clarified the cognition of my ears and eyes to govern the land. Leveling the flooded lands above, following the Long River below to the Mountain of Accounts, I spent ten years on waterworks. Now my limbs are useless and my home is broken up. How should I take care of this?"

Shi Gui replied, "The structure of government always begins with oneself. When blood and energy do not circulate as they should, this is called pathological blockage, which is the source of six extreme afflictions.

"The continuity of blood and energy, the coordination of the muscles and vessels, are not to be neglected. Let the brain relax, eat a varied diet; use intelligence for guidance, use work for exercise. Without food, there is no way to fill the stomach and develop the frame. Without intelligence, there is no way of discerning whether one is inwardly empty or full. Without work, there is no way to exercise the limbs to get rid of their afflictions.

"So, when you are going to sleep, draw your energy into your genitals; this is called exercising the tendons. Stretch and scrunch; this is called exercising the bones. Let your actions and functions be appropriate, and vitality will flow forth like a spring. In what age would this method not work?"

Now Yu took to drinking milk, and comforted his wife, so tranquillity was restored to his home.

This is Shi Gui's method of managing mind and energy.

9

WEN ZHI VISITED King Wei of Qi. King Wei asked him about the Way in these terms: "I have heard you are versed in the Way. Since I am already chief of state, I don't have time to listen to it all; I only want to hear one or two words about the essentials of the Way."

Wen Zhi replied, "I have composed three hundred essays on the Way, and sleeping is first and foremost."

King Wei asked, "Explain this. What should I eat at bedtime?"

Wen Zhi replied, "Fine wine and leeks."

King Wei asked, "Why do you recommend leeks?"

Wen Zhi replied, "When our ancestors practiced agriculture, they found leeks the only perennial herb, so they designated it as such. Leeks receive the energy of heaven early, and they receive the energy of earth fully. Therefore, if weakly and timid people eat leeks, they will be robust; if people whose eyes do not see well eat them, they will have clear vision. If people whose ears do not hear well eat them, they will have clear hearing. If you eat them for the three months of spring, sicknesses won't develop, and your tendons and bones will increase in strength. This is called the king of herbs."

King Wei said, "Good. And why do you recommend wine?"

Wen Zhi replied, "Wine is the vital energy of the five grains. When it enters the stomach, it disperses throughout the circulatory system, penetrating the physical structure and pervading it. It goes deeply into the system without requiring you to lie down and sleep. Therefore it is a vehicle for a hundred medicines."

King Wei said, "Good. But there is something that is not as you have said. When people suffering from dysentery in spring are given leeks, why are they given eggs instead of wine?"

Wen Zhi replied, "That will also do. Chickens are yang animals; their call at dawn is clear as they stretch their necks and spread their wings. During the three months of summer, chickens and leeks alike convey positive (yang) energy; that is why Taoists eat them."

King Wei said, "Good. Now why do you recommend sleep?"

Wen Zhi replied, "Sleep is not only a human activity. All birds, reptiles, fish, amphibians, and insects need food in order to live, and food needs sleep to work. Sleep enables food to be digested and disperses medicines to circulate through the body.

"Sleep is to food as fire is to gold. Therefore, if you do not sleep for one night, you will not recover for a hundred days. If food is not digested, it will be like having a ball in your gut. This produces listlessness and constipation, degeneration and debility. Therefore Taoists respect sleep."

King Wei said, "Good. If I always enjoy drinking from evening on into the night, will I not get sick?"

Wen Zhi replied, "No problem. Be like the birds and the beasts: those that go to sleep early rise early, those that go to sleep late rise late. The sky gets light, the earth gets dark; Taoists investigate those phenomena and go no further.

"The energy of food is absorbed subtly and circulated silently; during the night . . . energy is sent into all parts of the body. When all parts of the body are stably vitalized, you are inwardly solid while outwardly peaceful, so you don't get eruptions or tumors. This is the consummation of the Way."

King Wei said, "Good."

❧ 10 ❧

WHEN WANG QI made an appearance at court, King Zhao of Qin asked him about the Way in these terms: "I hear you ingest yin for active strength, and collect energy for vitality and clarity. What should I do to prolong my life?"

Wang Qi replied, "You must face the sun and the moon and collect their vital lights. Eat pine and cedar nuts, and drink the milk of running beasts. By these means you can fend off age and restore robustness, glowing with health. Avoid fire during the summer months, using a solar mirror to cook. Then the mind will be intelligent and bright.

"As for the way to engage in sexual intercourse, calmness makes for strength. Make the mind as calm as water, conserve the spiritual dew within. Knock at the jade door with the jade rod, the mind neither too tense nor too loose. You can tell what is best by how the woman sighs in response. Collect the spiritual mist, drink the celestial broth, sending them to the internal organs in order to store them deeply.

"Breathe gently in the mornings, and your energy and body will be firm . . . , vitality will be stable and long lasting. Peace of mind is attained within, the higher and lower thrive, the internal organs are stable, the complexion is lustrous. Life lasts as long as sun and moon, and you become a flower of heaven and earth."

King Zhao said, "Good."

JOINING YIN
AND YANG

1

GENERALLY SPEAKING, the way to initiate sexual intercourse is as follows. Hold hands, and begin stroking from the wrists, following the arms up to the armpits, then up to the shoulders and to the neck area. Stroke around the neck, then down to the hollow of the collarbone, over the nipples, across the belly, and up to the ribs. Reaching the vulva, massage the clitoris. Suck in energy to vitalize the spirit, and you can see forever and survive as long as the universe.

The clitoris is the vessel of intercourse inside the vulva; stroke it from below upward, causing the whole body to be pleasurably excited and the feelings to be joyfully delighted. Even though you want to, do not perform the act yet; hug and kiss, to loosen up and have fun.

The way to play is as follows. First, when energy rises and the face gets hot, slowly exhale. Second, when the woman's nipples become erect and her nose begins to run, slowly embrace. Third, when your tongues are sweet and slippery, slowly tongue kiss. Fourth, when her thighs are wet with her secretions, slowly move. Fifth, when her throat gets dry and she keeps swallowing saliva, slowly rock. These are called the five signs of desire.

When the five signs are all there, mount her and penetrate her, but do not go all the way in, so as to bring the energy. Once the energy comes, penetrate deeply and thrust upward into her, so as to disperse the heat. Repeat up and down movement, not letting the energy stop, and the woman will attain a great climax.

After that, perform ten sets of movements, continue with the ten styles of intercourse, and mix the ten manners of penetration. When sexual intercourse is finishing, concentrate the energy in the genitals, then watch the eight movements, listen to the five sounds, and observe the ten signs of consummation.

2

TEN SETS OF MOVEMENTS means ten times ten strokes: first ten, then twenty, then thirty, forty, fifty, sixty, seventy, eighty, ninety, one hundred. Withdraw and penetrate without ejaculating. Do one set without ejaculating, and your eyes and ears will be clear. Two sets, and your voice will be clear. Three, and your skin will be lustrous. Four, and your back and sides are strengthened. Five, and your buttocks and thighs get shaped up. Six, and your urinary tract will be clear. Seven, and your erection will be extremely firm and strong. Eight, and your skin will glow. Nine, and you join in a spiritual glow. Ten sets make the body endure.

The ten styles are as follows. First is called the tiger roaring. Second is called the cicada clinging. Third is called the inch-worm. Fourth is called the deer nudging with his antlers. Fifth is called the phoenix stretching. Sixth is called the monkey climbing. Seventh is called the toad. Eighth is called the rabbit running. Ninth is called the dragonfly. Tenth is called the fish feeding.

3

THE TEN MANNERS of penetration are as follows. First is stimulating the upper part of the female genitalia. Second is stimulating the lower part of the genitalia. Third is stimulating the left. Fourth is stimulating the right. Fifth is doing it rapidly. Sixth is doing it slowly. Seventh is doing it with low frequency. Eighth is doing it with high frequency. Ninth is doing it shallowly. Tenth is doing it deeply.

The eight movements are as follows. First is hugging, second is extending the arms, third is straightening the legs. Fourth is hooking the partner from the side with the legs, fifth is hooking the top, sixth is entwining the thighs. Seventh is level bouncing, eighth is vibration.

Hugging is for when you want your bellies touching. Extending the arms is done to stimulate the upper part of the woman's genitalia and continue for a long time. Straightening the legs is for when penetration is not deep enough. The woman hooks her legs around the man from the side when she wants stimulation of the sides of her genitalia; when she hooks her legs around the man above, she wants deep stimulation. Entwining the thighs is done when penetration is too deep. Level bouncing is for when shallow penetration is desired. Vibration occurs when the woman wants her man to continue for a long time.

Rapid breathing indicates inward urgency. Rough breathing indicates a climax. Sighing indicates the pleasure has begun after insertion of the jade rod. Heavy breathing indicates ecstasy. Nibbling and vibration of the body indicate that a woman wants her man to continue longer.

4

IN THE EVENINGS, male vitality is strong; in the mornings, female vitality has accumulated. When a male nurtures the female's vitality with his own vitality, the front vessels all get excited, the level of energy and blood in the skin rises; thus it is possible to open up what is closed and clear blockage, so the internal organs receive infusion and are replenished.

5

THE TEN SIGNS of consummation are as follows. At the first consummation, coolness emerges. At the second consummation, a smell like charred bone appears. The third consummation is characterized by heat. At the fourth consummation, there is an oil-like secretion. At the fifth consummation, a cereal-like fragrance appears. At the sixth consummation, there is so much lubrication as to be slippery. At the seventh consummation, there is prolongation. At the eighth consummation, the woman's secretion is like grease. At the ninth consummation, her secretion is sticky. At the tenth consummation, there is weakening, weakening followed by a return of slipperiness and a renewal of coolness. This is called the final finish.

Signs of the final finish are the woman's nose running and lips becoming pale, hands and feet trembling, buttocks rising off the bed. The man should stop now; it is harmful to wait until the erection disappears. At this time, the vulva is distended with energy, and the vital spirit enters the internal organs, where it produces an uncanny glow.

Talk on
Supreme Guidance
for the World

1

THE YELLOW EMPEROR asked the Spirit of the Left, "Yin and yang, the nine openings of the body, and the twelve major points are all born together, but the genitals alone 'die' or lose their function first. Why is this?"

The Spirit of the Left said, "Because the genitals are not employed in doing work. They are not instrumental in emotion, they do not help in eating and drinking; their abode is very hidden and not exposed to the sun, they are hastily and roughly used, they do not wait for maturity and cannot endure the friction of intercourse—therefore they wear out early. We avoid their names and hide their members, we use them most without restraint and without propriety; therefore they are born with the body but lose their individual function first."

2

IF AN ERECTION does not become large, that means the flesh is not energized. If an erection is not firm, that means the muscles are not energized. If it is firm but not hot, that means the mind is not energized.

If you use it when the flesh is not energized, the erection wilts. If you use it when the mind is not energized, the erection disappears. When all three are energized, that is called triple readiness.

[SECTION 3—NO TEXT]

4

LIKE WATER, darkly pervasive, like the energies of spring and autumn, as what has gone is not perceived, one cannot take advantage thereof; as what is yet to come is unseen, we look to what it presents. Be careful! This matter of the spiritual glow lies in stopping ejaculation. Operate the precious lock carefully, and the spiritual glow will arrive.

In general, physical cultivation calls for accumulation of vitality. When vitality is replete, it should be spent; and when vitality is wanting, it should be replenished. Replenishment of spent vitality is done when vitality is wanting.

In this practice, sit together, with your loins, noses, and mouths close together. If you go ahead suddenly and come precipitately, you will ejaculate uselessly and your vitality will be lost. How can one stop this? Emptying and filling have normal constants; employ them carefully and do not forget them. Avoid excessive fatigue, avoid exhaustion, and your sinews and bones will be strong. To continue, swallow saliva and take in fresh air. Exhale and inhale very gently, as a rule until you feel filled. When the energy of these three in harmony peaks, the result is firmness and strength.

If you want to master this, you must pay careful attention

to the instructions. By stopping the emission of semen, you can attain uncanny longevity. After one time, your eyes and ears are bright. A second time, and your voice is clear. A third time, and your skin is lustrous. A fourth time, and your spine is strengthened. A fifth time, and your buttocks and thighs are shaped up. A sixth time, and your urinary tract is clear. A seventh time, and your mind is firm and strong. An eighth time, and you are high-spirited. A ninth time, and you harmonize with heaven and earth. The tenth time produces the uncanny spiritual glow.

5

ENERGY HAS eight pluses and seven minuses. If you cannot employ the eight pluses and get rid of the seven minuses, then physical energy will diminish by half by the time you are forty; by fifty, your activities will decline; by sixty your hearing and vision will be unclear; and by seventy you will be withered below and debilitated above; sexual energy will not function, tears and mucus will run.

There is a way to restore strength: eliminate the seven minuses to quell afflictions, and use the eight pluses to enhance energy. Thus the aging can be restored to robustness, while the robust can avoid deterioration.

Educated people live in comfort and eat and drink what they want; their skin texture is fine, their energy and blood are full, their bodies are readily mobile. If they are too hasty in sexual intercourse, they cannot follow the proper course; this produces illness, sweating, gasping, internal disturbance, and mental confusion.

If you cannot cure this, you develop internal fever. Take herbs and moxacautery treatments to induce energy, take dietary supplements to enhance physical strength. If you force intercourse, without being able to follow the proper course, that will produce hemorrhoids and scrotal swelling; there is distention with energy and blood, dysfunction of bodily openings, debility in the upper and lower limbs, piles and ulcers. So use the eight pluses skillfully, eliminate the seven minuses, and these ailments will not occur.

THE EIGHT PLUSES are as follows. First is mastering energy. Second is producing moisture. Third is knowing the right timing. Fourth is accumulating energy. Fifth is gentle moistening. Sixth is building up energy. Seventh is maintaining fullness. Eighth is stabilizing the erection.

THE SEVEN MINUSES are as follows. First is shutting. Second is leaking. Third is exhaustion. Fourth is impotence. Fifth is emotional disturbance. Sixth is alienation. Seventh is waste.

8

TO MASTER THE eight pluses, rise at dawn, sit up, straighten your spine, relax your buttocks, contract your perineal muscles, and conduct energy to your sexual organs. This is called producing moisture.

When foreplay is mutually satisfactory, and both want to do it, that is called knowing the right timing.

During intercourse, let your back be relaxed, contract your perineal muscles, and exert pressure downward; this is called accumulating energy.

Do not go in and out too rapidly, or with too high frequency; glide in and out gently and with control. This is called gentle moistening.

When you are going to get out of bed, withdraw while you still have an erection; this is called building up energy.

When about finished, breathe deeply, avoid agitation, gather energy and press it down, waiting in a state of physical calm; this is called maintaining fullness.

When finished, wash off; withdraw while still erect. This is called stabilizing the erection.

These are called the eight pluses.

9

The seven minuses are as follows. When intercourse is painful, that is called inner shutting. Heavy perspiration and premature ejaculation during intercourse are referred to as external leaking. Hyperactivity means exhaustion. Inability in spite of desire is called impotence. Doing it breathlessly and inwardly out of control is called emotional disturbance. Forcing it when there is no desire means alienation. Doing it too fast means waste. These are called the seven minuses.

Therefore, if you skillfully employ the eight pluses and eliminate the seven minuses, your eyes and ears will be bright and clear, your body will be light and nimble, your sexual energy will grow stronger and stronger, you will extend your years, increasing your life span, and will live in lasting happiness.

❧ 10 ❧

HUMAN BEINGS are born able to do two things without learning how: one is breathing, the other is feeding. Everything other than these two things has to be learned and practiced. So, since nutrition enhances health while sensuality undermines health, wise people necessarily have rules for intercourse between men and women.

11

So, ONE IS "tigers rollicking," another is "cicada clinging," conscious of breathing externally. A third is "inchworm," a fourth is "deer raising antlers." Fifth is "phoenix spreading wings," conscious of breathing internally; sixth is "monkeys squatting," conscious of breathing externally. Seventh is "toads," eighth is "rabbits bounding." Ninth is "dragonflies," conscious of breathing externally, tenth is "fish feeding." These are called the ten postures.

The ten refinements are energizing, swallowing saliva, controlling the penis, stimulating the clitoris, making sure of proper timing, communing in intercourse, moving gently, awaiting fullness, climaxing together, and physically resting.

The eight ways are high, low, left, right, deep, shallow, fast, and slow.

Once you are ready for the ten refinements and prepared for the ten postures, have intercourse at night, using a variety of the eight ways. Before sweat flows, drive your energy into your genitals, hold your breath and make your pudenda vibrate, clearing the vessels and enhancing the ligaments. Watch for the woman's eight movements, observe where her energy is, and note how she moans and sighs, to decide what to do next.

12

HER EIGHT MOVEMENTS are hugging, pushing, stretching flat, straightening her legs, crossing thighs, vibrating, sideways hooking, upward hooking.

Her sounds are throaty breathing, panting, sighing, groaning, and nibbling. Observe her sounds carefully, to know her heart; observe her eight movements carefully, to know what she enjoys and what is effective.

When she hugs, she wants bellies touching; when she pushes, she wants isolated stimulation of the mons veneris. When she hooks her legs around the man from the side, she wants lateral stimulation. When she crosses her thighs, it means penetration is too deep; when she straightens her legs, it is not deep enough. When she hooks her legs around the man above, it means he hadn't penetrated all the way in. When she vibrates, it is supremely good. These are called the eight observations.

When energy rises and your faces get hot, slowly kiss. When her nipples erect and her nose runs, slowly embrace. When your tongues are thinly coated and slippery, slowly get together. When her thighs are wet with her secretions, slowly move. When her throat is dry and she swallows saliva, slowly rock. These are called the five signs. These refer to five expressions of desire. When all five are present, then you may initiate intercourse.

When an erection is not full-size, that means the flesh is not energized. When it is full-size but not hard, that means the muscle is not energized. When it is hard but not hot, that means the mood is not there. When all three are energized, then penetration is possible.

With one consummation, there appears a clear coolness. With the second consummation, there is a smell like charred bone. With the third consummation, there is a burning heat. With the fourth consummation, there is an oily secretion. With the fifth consummation, there is a grainlike aroma. With the sixth consummation, the sexual secretion is viscous. With the seventh consummation, it becomes sticky. With the eighth consummation, it becomes greasy. With the ninth consummation, it thickens. With the tenth consummation, there is a climax, climax and return of slipperiness; refreshed energy then emerges.

The opening and anterior chamber of the vulva, the outer and inner lips, the clitoris, the muscular entrance of the vagina, the vaginal walls, front and back, right and left, the entrance of the cervix: find them and keep them stimulated, finishing before losing erection. Drive the energy into the flesh and skin, and place it in the waist and inside of the body. The lips pale, sweat flows to the back of the knees; you are now counting strokes by the hundred.

13

A MAN WHO IS a good lover does not precede the woman; only when the woman has the desire can a good lover make love. Do not be precipitous, do not be domineering; do not force, but do not be hesitant. Make sure to be slow to prolong the act, and make sure to be gentle to maintain self-control, so you do not climax when on the brink of climax; then the woman will be greatly delighted.

Breathing through the open mouth expels negative energy and increases positive energy. Panting means respiration becomes rapid; now female genitalia open up. Sighing is accompanied by rapid movement of the buttocks to stimulate the labia. Groaning signals intense pleasure and the beginning of preorgasmic tension. Nibbling means she has climaxed and wants to go on longer.

So the male is categorized as yang, and yang is associated with the external, while the female is categorized as yin, and yin is associated with the internal. The stimulation of the male is on the outside, while the stimulation of the female is on the inside; this is called the logic of yin and yang, the reason of female and male. If it is done wrong, the fault is simply in the methodology.

What is essential in the pleasure between females and males is a matter of taking it slowly and continuing for a long time. If the man can go slowly and continue for a long time, the woman will be greatly delighted, feeling more friendly toward him than siblings do toward each other and more loving toward him than are parents toward their children. Those who are able to master the science are called celestial knights.

Courses in Effectiveness and Guidance

A Course in Effectiveness

Higher effectiveness is not ambitious;
    that is why it is effective.
Lower effectiveness does not forget reward,
    so it lacks efficacy.
When higher effectiveness is uncontrived,
    it has no ulterior motive;
higher benevolence is actively done,
    but has no ulterior motive.
When higher effectiveness is deliberately exercised,
    it is done for a purpose.
When higher courtesies are performed,
    yet no one responds to them,
    then they are repeated in an exaggerated manner.

Thus effectiveness is needed after guidance is lost,
    benevolence is needed after efficacy is lost,
    duty is needed after benevolence is lost,
    ritual is needed after duty is lost.
Ritual is thinness of faithfulness,
    and the beginning of disorder.

Advance knowledge is a result of guidance,
    but also the beginning of ignorance.
Therefore great people live by the thick,
    not the thin;
    they live by the substantial,
    not the superficial.
Thus they take one and leave the other.

The immemorial attainment of unity was thus:
    the sky attained unity,
    whereby it became clear;
    the earth attained unity,
    whereby it became steady;
    the spirit attained unity,
    whereby it became quickened;
    the valleys attained unity,
    whereby they were filled;
    leaders and rulers attained unity,
    whereby they became guides for the world.
Such is the extent of this that
    if the sky had no way to be clear,
    it would probably split;
    if the earth had no way to be steady,
    it would probably erupt;
    if the spirit had no way to be quickened,

it would probably wear out;
if the valleys had no way to be filled,
they would probably dry up;
if leaders and rulers had no way to be noble and lofty,
they would probably stumble.
So if you want to be noble,
it is rooted in humility;
if you want to be elevated,
it is based on lowering yourself.
This is why leaders and rulers call themselves
orphaned, isolated, and unlucky;
this is their use of humility as a basis, is it not?
Thus repeated elevation is no elevation,
so they don't want to be
shiny as jewels
but hard as stones.

When superior people hear guidance,
they diligently and ably carry it out.
When middling people hear guidance,
it is vague and uncertain.
When lesser people hear guidance,
they laugh.
If they didn't laugh at it,
it wouldn't be worth taking for guidance.

So there are established sayings:

> Guidance to enlightenment seems like nonsense,
> guidance to progress seems regressive,
> guidance to equality seems to classify.

Higher effectiveness seems at a loss,

> great purity seems like disgrace,
> broad-ranging effectiveness seems insufficient,
> constructive effectiveness seems to be casual.

Basic reality seems changeable,

> great expanse has no shores.
> A great vessel is completed late,
> a great sound is rarely heard.

The form of Nature is formless;

> guidance is concealed unnamed.
> But only guidance makes a good beginning
> and a good completion.

Guidance acts by return and renewal,

> and functions without force or aggression.

Everything in the world arises from being,

> being arises from nonbeing.

Guidance produces unity,

> unity produces division,

division produces synthesis,
  synthesis produces all things.
All things bear the negative and embrace the positive,
  with a tuning energy to harmonize them.
Everyone dislikes being orphaned, isolated, and unlucky,
  yet kings and lords refer to themselves this way.
So people may benefit from less,
  and may be harmed by more.
What others have to teach me
  is also what I have to teach others.
So even the powerful and clever cannot choose their death;
  I consider this the father of learning.

What is softest in the world
  drives what is hardest in the world;
  nonbeing penetrates even where there is no gap:
  by this I know the benefit of noncontrivance.
Unspoken instruction and uncontrived benefit
  are rarely reached in the world.

Which is dearer to you,
  your name or your body?
Which means more to you,
  your body or your goods?
Which afflicts you more,
  gain or loss?

When there is extreme craving,
    there is much expense;
    when there is much hoarded,
    there is a lot to lose.
Therefore, if you know when you have enough,
    you won't be disgraced;
    and if you know when to stop,
    you won't be endangered.
In this way you can live a long time.

Great achievement seems to be missing something,
    but its use is inexhaustible.
Great fulfillment seems empty,
    but its function is endless.
Great straightforwardness seems inarticulate,
    great skillfulness seems clumsy,
    great surplus is kept out of sight.
Movement overcomes cold,
    stillness overcomes heat;
    by clear calm,
    you can be correct in all worldly things.

When the world has guidance,
    chargers are sent back to manure the fields;
    when the world lacks guidance,
    war horses are bred in the countryside.

No mistake is worse than greed,
    no calamity is worse than discontent,
    no fault is more worrisome than
    desire for gain.
Therefore, the sufficiency of contentment
    is always enough.

Know the world
    without going out the door,
    know the weather
    without looking out the window.
The further out it goes,
    the less knowledge is;
    so sages know without going,
    name without seeing,
    create without contriving.

While those who strive to learn gain daily
    those who practice guidance lose daily,
    losing and even losing that,
    until they reach freedom from artificiality.
Having no artificiality,
    they can do anything.
Those who would take the world
    are always disinterested;

had they a stake in it,
they would be inadequate
to take the world.

Sage leaders are always mindless,
    using consciousness of all perceptions for mind.
They see the good in the good,
    and even in those who do not do well,
    they still see some good:
    this is finding the good.
They trust the trustworthy,
    and as for the unreliable,
    they trust them to be so:
    that is effective trust.

The presence of sage leaders in the world is conciliatory;
    they cloud their minds for the world,
    so all people are in their sight and hearing,
    and sage leaders include everyone,
    with an innocent smile.

We go forth into life and return in death.
There are thirteen associates of life,
    and thirteen associates of death.
But the life of the people creates a fuss

and all of them go
  to the thirteen grounds of death.
Why? Because they take living to be life.
It is said that those who hold on to life well
  do not avoid rhinos and tigers when traveling
    the highlands,
  do not don armor in the army;
  rhinos have no way to gore them,
  tigers have no way to claw them,
  weapons have no way to pierce them.
Why? Because there is no fatal spot in them.

Guidance creates, effectiveness nurtures,
  beings give shape, implements complete.
That is why all beings honor guidance and value
        effectiveness.
The nobility of guidance and the value of effectiveness
  are not bestowed by anyone,
  but naturally so of themselves.
Guidance creates, nurtures, develops, matures,
  brings to fruition, nourishes, sustains, and shelters.
It is creative without possessiveness,
  constructive without conceit,
  developmental without coerciveness;
  this is called unobtrusive effectiveness.

The world has a beginning
    that is the source of the world.
Once you find the source,
    you thereby know the product.
Once you know the product,
    go back to preserve the source,
    and you'll never be endangered.
Shut the openings, close the doors,
    and you'll never be belabored.
Open up the openings and manage affairs,
    and you'll never be saved.
Noticing the small is called clarity,
    keeping flexible is called strength.
Using the light,
    then return to clarity,
    and you leave nothing harmful.
This is called following the constant.

If we have any knowledge
    to practice great guidance,
    only deviation is to be feared.
Guidance is easy,
    but people are very obstinate.
When the courts are very tidy
    but the fields are very weedy

and the granaries very empty,
to wear colorful clothing
and carry sharp swords,
to eat to satiation
and possess excess wealth,
is called the arrogance of thieves.
The arrogance of thieves is no guide!

What is well built does not fall apart,
    what is well wrapped does not come loose;
    their inheritors pay them honor no end.
Develop it in the individual,
    and effectiveness is real;
develop it in the home,
    and effectiveness is more than enough.
Develop it in the community,
    and effectiveness grows;
develop it in the state,
    and effectiveness abounds.
Develop it all over the world,
    and effectiveness is universal.
See the individual as an individual,
    see the family as a family,
    see the community as a community,
    see the state as a state,
    see the world as a world.

How do I know the world is thus?
    That's how!

The depth of inner effectiveness
    is comparable to an infant,
    which bees, bugs, and snakes
    do not sting or bite,
    predatory birds and wild beasts
    do not snatch.
Its bones and tendons are weak and soft,
    yet its grip is firm;
it knows nothing of sexual intercourse,
    yet its organ erects:
    this is the epitome of vitality.
It can cry all day
    without getting hoarse;
    this is the epitome of harmony.
Harmony is called the constant;
    knowing the constant
    is called enlightenment.
Enhancing life is called auspicious;
    when the mind employs energy,
    that is called strength.
When beings peak in power, they age;
    this is called unguided.
The unguided soon perish.

Those who know do not say,
    those who say do not know.
Shut the openings, close the entryways;
    soften the light, merge with the dust;
    blunt the sharpness, unravel the complications.
This is called mystic sameness,
    by virtue of which you cannot be approached,
    yet cannot be estranged;
    you cannot be helped,
    and cannot be harmed;
    you cannot be valued
    and cannot be despised,
    and thus are noblest in the world.

Use convention to govern a state,
    use surprise in military action,
    use disinterest to take the world.
How do I know it is so?
When there are many taboos in the world,
    the people grow poorer and poorer.
When the people have many weapons,
    the nation grows more benighted.
When the people are very crafty,
    weird things arise more and more.
The greater the articulation of rules of law,
    the more brigands and outlaws there are.

Therefore a wise ruler says,

"If I do nothing,

the people will naturally be civilized.

If I am fond of quietude,

the people will naturally be upright.

If I am disinterested,

the people will naturally become rich.

If I want not to want,

the people will naturally be innocent."

When the administration is noninvasive,

the people are pure and simple.

When the administration is intrusive,

the people are lacking and wanting.

Disaster rests on fortune,

fortune is concealed in disaster.

Who knows the end? Is there nothing normal?

When the normal has become exceptional,

the good also becomes bad;

people's confusion is sure longstanding!

So be correct without being cutting,

be pure without being critical,

be straightforward without being oppressive,

be enlightened without being dazzling.

In government and religion both,
    it's best to be economical.
Only by being economical
    can order be promptly achieved.
This is called double buildup of effectiveness.
By double buildup of effectiveness,
    nothing is impossible.
When nothing is impossible,
    no limit can be determined.
When no limit can be determined,
    it is possible to have a state.
The matrix of having a state
    makes it possible to last.
This is called deepening the root.
    and solidifying the stem,
    the way to long life
    and enduring vision.

Govern a large state like cooking small fish;
    use guidance to construct the world.
Then spirits are not sacred.
Not that they are not sacred,
    but their supernatural powers
    do not hurt people.

Wise leaders also cause no harm.
Since neither hurts the other,
> their efficacies combine to reach the goal.

A great nation flows downward;
> female to the world,

> it is a meeting place for the world.

The female always overcomes the male by stillness.
When being still, it is appropriate to be lower.
Therefore, a great nation,
> by lowering itself to a small state,

> takes a small state.

A small state,
> by lowering itself to a great nation,

> takes from a great nation.

So one may take by being lower,
> or one may be taken from by the lower.

Thus a great nation
> only wants to include

> and nurture people;

a small state
> only wants to join

> and serve people.

For both to attain their desire,
> the great one should be lower.

Guidance is what keeps all things together;
    the treasure of good people,
    it is what protects people who are not good.
Fine works can be sold,
    reverential actions can burden people;
    even if people are no good,
    why would they abandon these?
Therefore when the ruler of all
    sets up the inner cabinet,
    though there be presentation
    of ceremonial jade insignia
    and teams of four horses,
    that is not as good
    as calmly proceeding
    with this guidance.
Why was this guidance valued of yore?
Is it not said that seekers find thereby,
    while those in error get free of it thereby?
Therefore it is what is most valuable in the world.

Act without contrivance,
    work without servility,
    savor the unflavored.
Make the small great,
    make the little much.
Respond to hatred with grace,
    plan for the difficult
    while it is still easy.

The greatest things in the world
 are done while still slight;
  so wise leaders never do big things,
  and thus can achieve greatness.
Those who agree too easily
 are inevitably little trusted;
  those who make things too easy
  are sure to have a lot of hardship.
Therefore wise leaders
 end up without difficulty
 by considering things hard.

It is easy to hold what's at rest,
 easy to plan for what hasn't come up.
It is easy to split what is frail,
 easy to dissolve what is slight.
Do it before it exists,
 govern it before it goes wild.
Enormous trees grow from sprouts,
 tall buildings rise from piles of earth,
 the loftiest heights start at your feet.
To contrive to do this is to spoil it;
 to try to cling to it is to lose it.
Therefore sages do not contrive anything,
 and thus do not spoil anything;
 they do not cling to anything,
 and thus do not lose anything.

People always fail in their business
  just as they are about to succeed;
  so be as careful of the end
  as you are of the beginning,
  and no business will fail.
Therefore sages want not to want,
  and do not value hard-to-get goods;
  they learn not to imitate,
  and reform the mistakes of the crowd.
They are able to assist the natural spontaneity of all beings,
  and do not dare to contrive artificialities.

The practice of guidance in ancient times
  was not to make people intellectual,
  but to make them innocent.
What makes people unruly
  is their cunning;
  so to govern a state by cunning
  is to undermine the state,
  while to govern a state by innocence
  is a blessing for the state.
To always be cognizant of these two
  is also a model for reflection;
  to always be cognizant of models for reflection
  is called hidden effectiveness.
Hidden effectiveness is deep, far-reaching;
  it is the opposite of things,
  but thus arrives at great accord.

The reason rivers and oceans
    can be kings of all valleys
    is because they are lower;
    that is how they can be kings
    of all valleys.
Therefore, when sages wish to rise above people,
    they lower themselves to them in their speech;
    when they want to lead people,
    they put themselves after them in status.
Thus people do not hurt them
    even though they are ahead;
    people do not consider them a burden
    even though they are on top.
Everyone in the world gladly promotes them
    without wearying of them.
Is it not because they are not contentious,
    so no one in the world can contend with them?

A small state has few people;
    it lets them have arms,
    but no one uses them;
    it lets them respect death
    and avoid moving away.
    They have boats and chariots
    but do not ride them;
    they have armor and weapons
    but do not deploy them.

It lets people go back to simple technology:
 they enjoy their food, like their clothing,
 enjoy their customs, are at peace in their homes.
The neighboring state may be so near
 that the cries of the chickens and dogs
 can be heard,
 yet the people have never been there
 in all their lives.

Truthful words are not prettified,
 prettified words are not truthful.
Those who know do not generalize,
 those who generalize do not know.
Quality is not quantity,
 quantity is not quality.
Sages do not accumulate anything,
 since they use it to help people;
 the more they themselves have,
 since it is given to others,
 the more their own abundance.
So the guidance of Nature
 is to help and not harm;
 guidance for people
 is to act beneficially
 and not be contentious.

All in the world think themselves great,
 but the great do not care;

indeed, only by not caring
can they be great—
if they cared about it,
eventually they'd become petty.
I always have three treasures,
which I keep and value:
first is kindness,
second is economy,
third is not presuming
to be at the head of the world.
By virtue of kindness, one can be brave;
by virtue of economy, one can be versatile;
by virtue of not presuming to be
at the head of the world,
one can become foremost
of successful functionaries.
Now, if you give up that kindness and courage,
if you give up that economy and versatility,
if you give up that humility and preeminence,
then you die.
If you go into battle with kindness,
then you will prevail;
use it for defense,
and you will be secure.
When Nature is going to establish people,
it seems to surround them with kindness.

So it is that good warriors are not militaristic,
    good fighters don't get angry,
    and those who are good at beating opponents
    do not get caught up in it.
Those who are good at employing people
    act as if they were under them;
    this is called the effectiveness
    of noncontention.
This is called employing people,
    this is called companionship with Nature;
    it is the ultimate attainment of time immemorial.

There are sayings about military operations:
    "We do not presume to initiate action,
    but we will defend."
    "We do not presume to advance an inch,
    and are willing to withdraw a foot."
This is called carrying out no maneuvers,
    shaking no fists, grabbing no weapons;
    that is how you get to have no enemies!
No calamity is greater than ignoring enemies;
    ignore enemies, and you are close
    to losing what you value.
So a warrior is unaffected by victory,
    and the compassionate one will prevail.

My sayings are very easy to recognize
    and easy to put into practice;
        yet no one in the world can recognize them,
    and no one can put them into practice.
The sayings have a source,
    the tasks have a master,
    only no one knows;
    that is why they don't know me.
Those who know me are rare;
    thus am I valuable.
So it is that wise people
    wear rough clothing
    concealing a treasure.

It is excellent to know innocently;
    it is sick to feign knowledge ignorantly.
The reason wise people are not sick
    is that they consider sickness sick;
    this is how they avoid sickness.

When people are not overawed,
    then is great awesomeness
    on the verge of perfection.
They do not have contempt for their houses,
    they do not tire of their livelihood.
Simply because they do not tire of them,
    they are not tiresome.

So it is that the wise know themselves
    but do not see themselves;
    they take care of themselves
    but do not exalt themselves.
Thus they leave one and take the other.

Courage in daring is murderous,
    courage in nonpresumption is life-giving;
    either may be helpful or harmful.
Who knows the reason
    for what Nature dislikes?
So the guidance of Nature
    is to win well without fighting,
    to respond well without anything being said,
    to come spontaneously without being called,
    to rebound with good strategies.
The network of Nature is vast,
    with large openings,
    yet lets nothing slip.

If the people were constant and conscientious
    but did not fear death,
    how could execution intimidate them?
If the people were constant and feared death,
    and whoever did anything eccentric
    you could capture and kill,
    who would dare?

When the people are constantly and inevitably
    fearful of death,
    then there are always executioners.
Those who kill in place of executioners
    are cutting in the carpenter's stead;
    and those who cut in the carpenter's stead
    rarely avoid hurting their hands.

When the people are starving,
    it is because they are too heavily taxed;
    this is why they starve.
When the peasants are unruly,
    it is because the leaders
    act for their own purposes;
    that is why there is disorder.
When people slight death,
    it is because of the intensity
    of their quest for life;
    this is why they slight death.
Only those who do not use life
    as a reason for artificialities
    are intelligently valuing life.

People are supple when they are born,
    and rigid when they die.
All beings, even plants and trees,
    are tender when born
    and brittle when they die.

So rigidity is the associate of death,
    suppleness is the associate of life.
When militarists are strong,
    they do not win;
    when trees are strong,
    they are resistant.
So the powerful giants are lower,
    while flexible weaklings are higher.

Nature's guidance is like drawing a bow:
    it lowers the high
    and raises the low,
    reduces surplus
    and increases what is lacking.
The way of humans
    is to take from the have-nots
    and give it to the haves.
Who can have a surplus
    and have a way to derive from it
    service of Nature?
    Only one who is guided, it seems.
Therefore sages act without possessiveness
    and succeed without conceit.
    They are thus because
    they do not want to appear wise.

Nothing in the world
    is more yielding than water,

yet nothing can outstrip it
    in attacking the hard and the strong;
    that is because nothing can change it.
Everyone in the world knows
    water can overcome what is hard,
    and yielding can overcome strength,
    yet no one can practice this.
Therefore sages say
    that one who accepts
    the criticism of the nation
    is lord of the land;
    one who accepts
    the ill fortune of the nation
    is lord of the world.
True sayings seem paradoxical.

When you harmonize great enemies
    yet bitterness is sure to remain,
    how can that be considered good?
So wise people keep their end of an agreement
    and do not put the pressure on others;
    the effective take responsibility for promises,
    the ineffective take charge of exactions.
The guidance of Nature is impartial;
    it is always there for good people.

A Course in Guidance

Guidance can be articulated,
>   but not in an unchanging course;
>   terms can be defined,
>   but not a fixed terminology.
Nonbeing is called the beginning of all things,
>   being is called the mother of all things.
Therefore, constant passionlessness
>   is used to observe the subtle,
>   while constant intent
>   is used to observe what it calls.
These two come from the same source
>   but have different names;
>   this is called the mystery of mysteries,
>   the gateway of subtleties.

When everyone recognizes "beauty"
>   as beauty, this is bad.
>   When everyone recognizes "good,"
>   this is not good.
Affirmation and negation produce each other,
>   difficulty and ease complement each other,

long and short form each other,
high and low fulfill each other,
thought and voice conform to each other,
before and after follow each other—
these are constants.
Therefore wise people live without artificiality
and act on unspoken teaching;
everything starts without their initiative,
they act without dependence,
succeed without conceit.
Only by not being conceited about it
do they thereby avoid its loss.

To refrain from exalting cleverness
gets the people not to compete.
To refrain from valuing hard-to-get goods
gets the people not to be thieves.
To refrain from seeing the desirable
gets the people not to go wild.
So the government of wise leaders
empties the mind and fills the middle,
weakens ambitions and strengthens bones,
always making the people innocent, not greedy.
They cause the sophisticated not to be daring;
they do not contrive artificialities,
that is all—so nothing is out of order.

Guidance is open-ended,
    so its application has no limit;
    it is so deep it seems to be
    the source of all things.
Blunt sharp edges,
    unravel tangles,
    harmonize enlightenment,
    assimilate to the world.
Submerged in the depths,
    it seems it may be there;
    I don't know whose offspring it is,
    before the creation of forms.

Sky and earth are inhuman;
    to them, all beings are straw dogs.
    When rulers are not humane,
    they treat the peasants like straw dogs.
The space between sky and earth, like a bellows,
    is empty yet never exhausted,
    producing more with movement.
Formal learning runs out of resources
    time and time again;
    it does not compare
    to keeping to the center.

Purify the spirit,
    and you won't be morbid;

this is called the opening
of the mystic feminine.
The mystic feminine is called
the root of the universe;
a subtle continuity,
it is indeed there;
apply it without stress.

The sky lasts,
the earth endures.
The reason sky and earth
are lasting and enduring
is that they do not foster themselves;
therefore they can live long.
So sages withdraw themselves
and thereby take the lead;
they exclude themselves
and thereby survive.
Is it not because of their unselfishness
that they are able to attain their own interests?

Higher good is like water:
water benefits all beings,
and also rests quietly
where most people dislike to be;
thus it approximates guidance.

Goodness of abode is location;
    goodness of heart is depth;
    goodness of foresight is natural;
    goodness of speech is trustworthiness.
Goodness of government is order;
    goodness of work is capability;
    goodness of action is timeliness.
But only by noncontention
    can you be impeccable.

To keep filling is not as good as stopping;
    a sharpened point can't be kept permanent;
    though gold and jade fill their houses,
    no one can keep them secure.
The upper-class rich who are haughty
    leave a legacy of blame;
    to retire when your work is done
    is the guiding way of Nature.

Honoring the creative spirit,
    yet embracing oneness,
    can you avoid alienation?
Concentrating energy,
    making it flexible,
    can you be childlike?
Cleaning the mirror

of subtle perception,
    can you make it flawless?
Caring for the people,
    governing the nation,
    can you do it without cunning?
As the doors of Nature
    open and close,
    can you be receptive?
As clear understanding
    reaches everywhere,
    can you remain innocent?
Creating and developing,
    creating without possessiveness,
    promoting without domineering;
        this is called unobtrusive effectiveness.

Thirty spokes, the same one hub;
    where there is nothing
    is the function of the wheel.
When you work clay into a vessel,
    where there is nothing
    is the function of the clay vessel.
When you open up doors and windows,
    it is where there is nothing
    that the room is functional.

So you have something for its benefit,
 and have nothingness for its function.

Colors make people's eyes blind,
 racing and hunting
 craze people's minds.
Hard-to-get goods
 make people's behavior erratic,
 spices confuse people's palates,
 sounds deafen people's ears.
So the government of sages
 is for the gut,
 not for the eye:
 they leave the latter
 and take the former.

Favor and disgrace startle you;
 high status greatly afflicts your person.
What does it mean to say
 that favor and disgrace startle you?
Favor is the lower:
 gain it, and you are startled;
 lose it, and you are startled.
This means favor and disgrace startle you.
What does it mean to say
 that high status greatly afflicts your person?

The reason we have so much trouble
    is because we are so personal;
    if we were impersonal,
    what troubles would we have?
So how can the world be entrusted
    to those who hope to work for the world
    for their own personal interests?
How can the world be entrusted
    to those who like to work for the world
    for their own personal reasons?

What is invisible when you look
    is called subtle.
What is inaudible when you listen
    is called rarefied.
What is ungraspable to the touch
    is called forever constant.
These three are incalculable,
    so they are combined into one.
The one is not confused above
    and not indistinct below;
    an unbroken continuity,
    it cannot be named,
    reverting again to abstraction.

This is called
    the formless state,
    the image of the abstract.
This is called undefined:
    even if your gaze follows it,
    you cannot see its back;
    even if you go out to meet it,
    you do not see its head.
Hold to guidance for the present
    to control what presently exists,
    thus to know the perennial origin;
    this is called the guiding rule.

Those who applied guidance well of yore
    were subtle, mysterious,
    with inexplicable mastery,
    so deep they were inscrutable.
Only because of their inscrutability
    were they powerful.
To describe them, I would say
    they were hesitant,
    as if crossing a river in winter;
    they were prudent,
    as if wary of all around;

they were dignified,
　　as if they were guests;
they were diffuse,
　　like seeping moisture;
they were simple,
　　like uncarved wood;
they were deep,
　　like impenetrable waters;
they were wide open,
　　like enormous valleys.
When things are murky,
　　quiet down,
　　and they will gradually clear;
　　proceed,
　　and momentum gradually builds.
Those who keep this guidance
　　do not want oversatiation;
　　so they can use things to the full
　　and not keep making them.

Achieving openness is attainment,
　　keeping calm is mastery:
　　as everything acts in concert,
　　I use these to watch their return.

For beings, in all their variety, each returns;
  going back to the root is called calm—
  this is called return to life.
Return to life is perennial;
  to know the perennial is enlightenment.
  Not to know the perennial is confusion;
  the confused cause harm.
Know the perennial, and you are openminded;
  openmindedness is impartial fairness,
  impartial fairness is the highest nobility,
  the highest nobility is Nature itself.
Nature is guidance itself;
  guidance is eternal,
  never exhausted in all your life.

Great leaders are only known to exist,
  the next best are fondly praised;
  next after those are feared,
  while the lowest are despised,
  for they are not trusted enough.
When there is distrust,
  it stems from the high value
  that is placed on talk.
Accomplishing work,
  conducting their affairs,

the common people all think
it happens by nature.

So it is when universal guidance is abandoned
    that there are "humanity" and "duty."
When knowledge emerges,
    then there is great artificiality.
When relatives are out of harmony,
    then there are "obedience" and "kindness."
When a state is benighted and confused,
    then there are "virtuous ministers."

Eliminate repute and abandon recognition,
    and the people benefit a hundredfold.
Eliminate "humanitarianism" and abandon "duty,"
    and the people return to obedience and kindness.
Eliminate cleverness and abandon profiteering,
    and thieves and robbers will not exist.
Even these three sayings
    are due to lack in the culture,
    to which reference must be made.
Seeing the basic,
    embrace simplicity,
    reduce selfishness,
    and minimize cravings.

Even without formal learning there is no trouble:
    How far apart are "hello" and "hey"?
    How far apart are like and dislike?
Those whom others fear
    cannot but fear others;
    how shameful their imbalance!
Most people are raucous,
    like when they barbecue
    and sightsee in spring.
I am quiet, giving no sign,
    like a baby that hasn't smiled,
    restrained, as if belonging nowhere.
Most people have extra;
    I have the heart of a simpleton,
    without elaboration, uncomplicated.
Most people are bright;
    I alone am dim.
Most people are nosy;
    I alone am reserved,
    unfathomable as the ocean,
    with an endless perspective.
Most people have motives;
    I alone stand by the door of potential
    with nothing to cause abasement:
    my desire is unique, different from others;
    I value feeding from the source.

The capacity for great effectiveness
    only goes along with guidance.
Concretely, guidance is undefinable,
    but though it is undefinable,
    there are images in it;
    though it is undefinable,
    there is something to it.
Mysterious and impenetrable,
    there is vitality in it;
    that vitality is very real,
    having truth in it.
Henceforth and forever,
    this is called undeparting,
    as it goes along with all beginnings.
How do I know all beginnings are so?
    By this.

Blowhards cannot stand;
    those who look at themselves
    are not illustrious,
    those who see themselves
    are not enlightened.
    The arrogant are unsuccessful,
    the conceited do not grow.
    In the course of life,

these are called excess consumption
and exaggerated behavior;
people may dislike that,
so one who has cravings
should not dwell on them.

Be indirect for safety,
be roundabout for accuracy;
when depressed, you will be replenished,
when exhausted, you will be renewed.
Less is gain, more is confusion;
therefore sage leaders hold to oneness
in practicing governorship of the world:
They do not look at themselves,
so they are distinguished;
they do not see themselves,
so they are enlightened.
They are not arrogant,
so they are successful;
they are not conceited,
so they can grow.
Simply because they do not contend,
no one can contend with them.
The ancient saying,
"Be indirect for safety"

is a subtle saying indeed—
that's what sincerity is all about.

It is natural to speak little;
    a gale does not last all morning,
    a rainstorm does not last all day.
Who does this? Sky and earth.
    And even they cannot keep it up forever;
    how much less can humans!
So those who work on guidance
    identify with guidance;
    the effective identify with effectiveness,
    losers identify with losing.
Those who identify with effectiveness
    are also rewarded by guidance,
    while those who identify with losing
    are also lost to guidance.

There is something undifferentiated
    prior to the origin of sky and earth;
    inaccessible, utterly silent,
    independent and unchanging,
    it can be considered
    the matrix of the universe.
I do not know its name;
    I entitle it the guiding way.

I insist on calling it great,
    in the sense of having outreach,
    outreach in the sense of wide application,
    wide application that gets back to basics.
Guidance is important,
    the mental atmosphere is important,
    the physical environment is important,
    and leadership is important.
There are four important things to a nation,
    and leadership is one of them.
People are conditioned by the physical environment,
    the physical environment is conditioned
    by the mental atmosphere.
The mental atmosphere is conditioned by guidance,
    guidance is conditioned by inherent adaptiveness.

Gravity is the root of levity,
    calm is the ruler of excitement;
    by these means, cultured people
    may travel all day
    without leaving their equipment behind.
Even if they have a high office
    and a secure abode,
    they remain aloof.
What can be done
    about monarchs of great power

who slight the world
on their own personal account?
By levity,
they lose the root;
by excitement,
they lose sovereignty.

A skilled traveler leaves no tracks,
a skilled speaker makes no mistakes,
a skilled calculator needs no markers.
What is skillfully closed
has no lock,
yet cannot be opened.
What is skillfully bound
cannot be untied
though there is no binding rope.
So sages always skillfully save people
and never abandon people,
and never abandon what's useful in things;
this is called extension of enlightenment.
So good people are teachers of good people,
and people who are not good
are the raw material of good people.
If you do not value the teachers
and do not care for the raw material,

even if you are knowledgeable
you are very confused;
this is called an essential subtlety.

Knowing the masculine,
    preserve the feminine;
    be receptive to the world,
    and consistent effectiveness remains,
    returning to innocence.
Knowing purity,
    preserve ignominy;
    be always open to the world,
    and consistent effectiveness will be sufficient,
    returning again to simplicity.
Knowing the white,
    preserve the black,
    as a model for the world,
    and consistent effectiveness
    will not go away,
    returning again to infinity.
When a whole is diversified,
    there are specific functions;
    when sages are employed,
    they become officers and leaders.
    But there is no divisiveness
    in the overall system.

Generals want to take the world,
>   and even try to do it;
>   as I see it, they cannot.

For the world is a subtle instrument,
>   not something for which one can try.
>   Those who try for it spoil it;
>   those who grasp it lose it.

Things may go and may follow,
>   may heat and may shatter,
>   may expand and may collapse;
>   so the sage avoids the extreme,
>   avoids the grandiose,
>   avoids the extravagant.

Those who assist human leaders with guidance
>   do not coerce the world with weaponry;
>   these things are apt to backfire—
>   where armies dwell, brambles grow.

Experts are effective, that is all;
>   they do not use it to take power.

Effective without arrogance,
>   effective without conceit,
>   effective without pride,
>   they are effective from having no choice.

To abide in this is called
>   effectiveness without coerciveness.

When beings peak in strength,
    they age; this is called unguided.
    The unguided die prematurely.

Weapons are inauspicious tools;
    people may dislike them,
    so those with desires
    do not dwell on them.
At home, cultured people esteem the left,
    at war they esteem the right;
    so weapons are not the tools
    of cultured people.
Weapons are ill-starred implements;
    using them only when unavoidable,
    it is best to remain aloof
    and not glorify warfare.
If you glorify warfare,
    you are gladly killing people;
    if you gladly kill people,
    you cannot thereby
    gain your will in the world.
So auspicious events elevate the left,
    while mournful events elevate the right;
    thus the assistant commanders are on the left
    while the top generals are on the right,
    meaning their positions are as at funerals.

When the slain are many,
>   weep for them with sadness;
>   when you have won a war,
>   observe the occasion
>   with rites of mourning.

Guidance is always anonymous;
>   it is uncomplicated and minimal,
>   but no one in the world
>   dares presume to administer it.
>   If lords and kings could observe it,
>   everyone would resort to them.
Sky and earth combine
>   to rain sweet dew;
>   without the people causing it,
>   it is naturally even.
Begin organizing, and you have titles;
>   once you even have titles,
>   you should know when to stop;
>   knowing when to stop
>   is how to avoid endangerment.
The existence of guidance
>   in the world
>   is like the little ravine
>   feeding the rivers and seas.

Those who know others are intelligent,
>   those who know themselves are enlightened.
>   Those who overcome others are forceful,
>   those who overcome themselves are strong.
Those who are content are rich,
>   those who act with strength have will.
>   Those who do not lose their place endure,
>   those who die but aren't forgotten are immortal.

Guidance is universal;
>   it can be adapted
>   to higher or lower aims.
When it has completed an accomplishment
>   and finished a task,
>   it is no longer said to be there.
Everyone resorts to it,
>   but it does not try to control them,
>   so it is consistent, without desire;
>   this can be called minimal.
Everyone resorts to it,
>   but it does not try to control them;
>   this can be called magnanimous.
So the reason wise people
>   are able to achieve greatness
>   is that they don't consider it big;
>   that enables them to accomplish a lot.

When it holds to universal images,
> the world goes on and on without harm,
> its security and peace are great.

Where there is music and food
> is where passing tourists stop;
> so the utterances of guidance
> are plain and flavorless.

When you look at it,
> it cannot be seen;
> when you listen for it,
> it cannot be heard;
> when you apply it,
> it cannot be exhausted.

When you want to contain something,
> you should purposely let it expand;
> when you want to weaken something,
> you should purposely let it grow strong.

When you want to get rid of something,
> you should purposely go along with it;
> when you want to take something away,
> you should deliberately cede it.

This is called subtle enlightenment;
> flexibility and yielding overcome strength.

Fish are not to be taken from the pond,

efficient tools of a nation
are not to be shown to others.

Guidance is consistent,
     though undefinable;
     if lords and monarchs could keep to it,
     everything would be spontaneously orderly.
Though orderly,
     if they craved action,
     I would calm them down
     with undefinable simplicity.
Undefinable simplicity is a means
     of avoiding disgrace.
     Be serene by avoiding disgrace,
     and heaven and earth will right themselves.

Notes

Ten Questions

1. The Yellow Emperor is believed to have assumed leadership in 2697 BCE. *Celestial Teacher* refers to a Taoist adept; later it came to be used as a title for the head of a certain Taoist sect.

When these texts speak of taking or sending or driving energy into specific places, such as the skin or other organs, the reference is to coordinating breathing, feeling, movement, and attention in visualization or sensing exercises designed to enhance pleasure and health benefits.

3. Closing off the flow of semen is not permanent; it is done temporarily to avoid depletion and loss of sexual energy, thus enhancing potency and the ability to prolong the act. The "locking up" may here refer to muscular contraction to prevent ejaculation, as it later undoubtedly did; the emphasis here on the "watching over" may indicate, however, more focus on self-control through mindfulness and relaxation. The method of intense muscular contraction also has the function of initiating the ascent of energy up the spine in the standard Taoist "brain repair" exercise utilizing the orgasmic energy of sexual

intercourse; the timing of its application, however, is more problematic than mindfulness and relaxation, and like other physical exercises can have harmful side effects if practiced too intensely. In view of the absence of mention of more radical methods of "locking up" such as were later developed, and the presence of the specific recommendation of "peaceful serenity of heart" in the same connection, one guess is that the text here refers to a balanced combination of mental and muscular control.

4. "Sweet dew" is commonly thought to mean saliva, which is highly valued in Taoist hygiene and health lore. One exercise involves accumulating a mouthful of saliva, then swallowing it in three swallows, each time visualizing the saliva as a sweet dew or precious elixir bathing and nurturing the inner organs. The collecting of sweet dew can also refer to conservation of sexual energy through the scrupulous observance of the bedroom arts; this is suggested by the association with vitality.

5. Yao and Shun were both legendary wise kings of old. Yao is supposed to have reigned for a hundred years, from 2357 to 2257 BCE; Shun, who succeeded him, is supposed to have reigned from 2255 to 2207 BCE. "Care, education, consideration, and nutrition" is a good summary of the Huang-Lao approach to sexuality.

6. Peng Zu is believed to have lived eight hundred years; his name is associated with arts of longevity, especially sexual arts connected with longevity.

7. Pan Geng was a legendary prehistoric chieftain.

8. Yu was a sage king who succeeded Shun; he is supposed to have reigned from 2205 to 2197 BCE.

9. King Wei ruled the state of Qi from 356 to 320 BCE.

10. King Zhao ruled the state of Qin from 306 to 251 BCE.

JOINING YIN AND YANG

2. The ten styles of sexual intercourse mentioned here and again in the following treatise do not exactly correspond to those described in later lore, and are not all quite clear. In the tiger style, the woman crouches on hands and knees like a tiger, with arched back, while the man crouches on his knees behind her, embracing her around the waist and penetrating her from behind. In the cicada style, the woman lies flat on her belly with her legs outstretched; the man kneels between her thighs and enters her from behind. The inchworm style apparently refers to an imitation of the inchworm's alternate bending and straightening. In the deer nudging with his antlers, the man sits with his legs out, while the woman sits on his thighs with her back to his chest; as he holds her around the waist, he thrusts up into her from below. In the phoenix stretching style, the woman lies on her back and draws up her legs; the man kneels between her thighs, with his hands on the bed, and penetrates deeply into her. In the monkey climbing style, the man sits with his legs out, while the woman sits on his thighs facing him; with one hand on the bed for balance,

he holds the woman's buttock with the other as he enters her. The rabbit and toad styles are not clear. In the dragonfly style, the woman lies face down with the man lying face down on top of her. In the fish feeding style, the man lies on his back, while the woman crouches on top of him, drawing his penis inside her the way an infant sucks the mother's nipple.

3. "Extending the arms is done to stimulate the upper part of the woman's genitalia and continue for a long time" means that the woman extends her arms, pushing the man's upper torso away from her, or that the man extends his arms, pushing his upper body away from her, resulting in a more acute angle of contact between pudenda. This pressure not only intensifies the woman's pleasure through greater stimulation of the entire area but also helps the man control himself. Increased muscular exertion in this posture also helps male control, thus facilitating "continuing for a long time."

"Entwining the thighs is done when penetration is too deep," to restrict the degree of penetration. If the woman has a relatively prominent or highly placed mons, she may entwine her own thighs to achieve this effect. If the woman's mons is not prominent, or its location on her body is low in comparison to the rise of her thighs from the torso, the effect of limiting penetration may be achieved more comfortably by entwining her legs around the man's calves without spreading her thighs very much. In either case, the effect is to concentrate the stimulation in the area of the woman's mons, labia, and vaginal opening.

In "level bouncing," the man and woman may be thigh to thigh, with legs only slightly spread, gently pushing or "bouncing" against one another with bodies outstretched as they couple; or the man may suspend himself over the woman by his elbows and toes, making his body like a spring that lightly "bounces" in such a way as to stimulate the mons with a repeated massaging action while maintaining a continuous shallow penetration.

5. "Consummation" here involves a female climax but not a male orgasm; each climax or consummation refers to a complete act of love, while the man's orgasm is reserved for the "final finish."

Talk on Supreme Guidance for the World

1. The Spirit of the Left was evidently a title for a wizard employed by a royal court.

Bibliography

Lung Yi-yin. *Chung-kuo ku-tai hsing hsueh hi-cheng.* Hong Kong: Pa-lung Ch'u-pan Wen-hua Fu-wu Yu-hsien Kung-ssu, 1991.

Nan Huaichin. *Lao-tzu t'a-shuo.* Taipei: Lao-ku Wen-hua Shi-yeh Kung-ssu, 1988.

Zhou Yimou. *Mawangdui Han mu chu tu Fangzhong Yangsheng zhuozuo shiyao.* Beijing: Jinri Zhongguo Chubanshe, 1990.

Printed in the United States
by Baker & Taylor Publisher Services